# This planner belongs to :

_____

# 2026

## January

| S | M | T | W | T | F | S |
|---|---|---|---|---|---|---|
|   |   |   |   | 1 | 2 | 3 |
| 4 | 5 | 6 | 7 | 8 | 9 | 10 |
| 11 | 12 | 13 | 14 | 15 | 16 | 17 |
| 18 | 19 | 20 | 21 | 22 | 23 | 24 |
| 25 | 26 | 27 | 28 | 29 | 30 | 31 |

## February

| S | M | T | W | T | F | S |
|---|---|---|---|---|---|---|
| 1 | 2 | 3 | 4 | 5 | 6 | 7 |
| 8 | 9 | 10 | 11 | 12 | 13 | 14 |
| 15 | 16 | 17 | 18 | 19 | 20 | 21 |
| 22 | 23 | 24 | 25 | 26 | 27 | 28 |

## March

| S | M | T | W | T | F | S |
|---|---|---|---|---|---|---|
| 1 | 2 | 3 | 4 | 5 | 6 | 7 |
| 8 | 9 | 10 | 11 | 12 | 13 | 14 |
| 15 | 16 | 17 | 18 | 19 | 20 | 21 |
| 22 | 23 | 24 | 25 | 26 | 27 | 28 |
| 29 | 30 | 31 |   |   |   |   |

## April

| S | M | T | W | T | F | S |
|---|---|---|---|---|---|---|
|   |   |   | 1 | 2 | 3 | 4 |
| 5 | 6 | 7 | 8 | 9 | 10 | 11 |
| 12 | 13 | 14 | 15 | 16 | 17 | 18 |
| 19 | 20 | 21 | 22 | 23 | 24 | 25 |
| 26 | 27 | 28 | 29 | 30 |   |   |

## May

| S | M | T | W | T | F | S |
|---|---|---|---|---|---|---|
|   |   |   |   |   | 1 | 2 |
| 3 | 4 | 5 | 6 | 7 | 8 | 9 |
| 10 | 11 | 12 | 13 | 14 | 15 | 16 |
| 17 | 18 | 19 | 20 | 21 | 22 | 23 |
| 24 | 25 | 26 | 27 | 28 | 29 | 30 |
| 31 |   |   |   |   |   |   |

## June

| S | M | T | W | T | F | S |
|---|---|---|---|---|---|---|
|   | 1 | 2 | 3 | 4 | 5 | 6 |
| 7 | 8 | 9 | 10 | 11 | 12 | 13 |
| 14 | 15 | 16 | 17 | 18 | 19 | 20 |
| 21 | 22 | 23 | 24 | 25 | 26 | 27 |
| 28 | 29 | 30 |   |   |   |   |

## July

| S | M | T | W | T | F | S |
|---|---|---|---|---|---|---|
|   |   |   | 1 | 2 | 3 | 4 |
| 5 | 6 | 7 | 8 | 9 | 10 | 11 |
| 12 | 13 | 14 | 15 | 16 | 17 | 18 |
| 19 | 20 | 21 | 22 | 23 | 24 | 25 |
| 26 | 27 | 28 | 29 | 30 | 31 |   |

## August

| S | M | T | W | T | F | S |
|---|---|---|---|---|---|---|
|   |   |   |   |   |   | 1 |
| 2 | 3 | 4 | 5 | 6 | 7 | 8 |
| 9 | 10 | 11 | 12 | 13 | 14 | 15 |
| 16 | 17 | 18 | 19 | 20 | 21 | 22 |
| 23 | 24 | 25 | 26 | 27 | 28 | 29 |
| 30 | 31 |   |   |   |   |   |

## September

| S | M | T | W | T | F | S |
|---|---|---|---|---|---|---|
|   |   | 1 | 2 | 3 | 4 | 5 |
| 6 | 7 | 8 | 9 | 10 | 11 | 12 |
| 13 | 14 | 15 | 16 | 17 | 18 | 19 |
| 20 | 21 | 22 | 23 | 24 | 25 | 26 |
| 27 | 28 | 29 | 30 |   |   |   |

## October

| S | M | T | W | T | F | S |
|---|---|---|---|---|---|---|
|   |   |   |   | 1 | 2 | 3 |
| 4 | 5 | 6 | 7 | 8 | 9 | 10 |
| 11 | 12 | 13 | 14 | 15 | 16 | 17 |
| 18 | 19 | 20 | 21 | 22 | 23 | 24 |
| 25 | 26 | 27 | 28 | 29 | 30 | 31 |

## November

| S | M | T | W | T | F | S |
|---|---|---|---|---|---|---|
| 1 | 2 | 3 | 4 | 5 | 6 | 7 |
| 8 | 9 | 10 | 11 | 12 | 13 | 14 |
| 15 | 16 | 17 | 18 | 19 | 20 | 21 |
| 22 | 23 | 24 | 25 | 26 | 27 | 28 |
| 29 | 30 |   |   |   |   |   |

## December

| S | M | T | W | T | F | S |
|---|---|---|---|---|---|---|
|   |   | 1 | 2 | 3 | 4 | 5 |
| 6 | 7 | 8 | 9 | 10 | 11 | 12 |
| 13 | 14 | 15 | 16 | 17 | 18 | 19 |
| 20 | 21 | 22 | 23 | 24 | 25 | 26 |
| 27 | 28 | 29 | 30 | 31 |   |   |

# Year in Pixels

| | J | F | M | A | M | J | J | A | S | O | N | D |
|---|---|---|---|---|---|---|---|---|---|---|---|---|
| 1. | | | | | | | | | | | | |
| 2. | | | | | | | | | | | | |
| 3. | | | | | | | | | | | | |
| 4. | | | | | | | | | | | | |
| 5. | | | | | | | | | | | | |
| 6. | | | | | | | | | | | | |
| 7. | | | | | | | | | | | | |
| 8. | | | | | | | | | | | | |
| 9. | | | | | | | | | | | | |
| 10. | | | | | | | | | | | | |
| 11. | | | | | | | | | | | | |
| 12. | | | | | | | | | | | | |
| 13. | | | | | | | | | | | | |
| 14. | | | | | | | | | | | | |
| 15. | | | | | | | | | | | | |
| 16. | | | | | | | | | | | | |
| 17. | | | | | | | | | | | | |
| 18. | | | | | | | | | | | | |
| 19. | | | | | | | | | | | | |
| 20. | | | | | | | | | | | | |
| 21. | | | | | | | | | | | | |
| 22. | | | | | | | | | | | | |
| 23. | | | | | | | | | | | | |
| 24. | | | | | | | | | | | | |
| 25. | | | | | | | | | | | | |
| 26. | | | | | | | | | | | | |
| 27. | | | | | | | | | | | | |
| 28. | | | | | | | | | | | | |
| 29. | | | | | | | | | | | | |
| 30. | | | | | | | | | | | | |
| 31. | | | | | | | | | | | | |

## Color Codes

## Notes

# January 2026

| MONDAY | TUESDAY | WEDNESDAY | THURSDAY |
|---|---|---|---|
| | | | 1 |
| 5 | 6 | 7 | 8 |
| 12 | 13 | 14 | 15 |
| 19 | 20 | 21 | 22 |
| 26 | 27 | 28 | 29 |

# January

## 2026

| FRIDAY | SATURDAY | SUNDAY | NOTES |
|---|---|---|---|
| 2 | 3 | 4 | ○ |
|  |  |  | ○ |
|  |  |  | ○ |
|  |  |  | ○ |
|  |  |  | ○ |
| 9 | 10 | 11 | ○ |
|  |  |  | ○ |
|  |  |  | ○ |
|  |  |  | ○ |
|  |  |  | ○ |
| 16 | 17 | 18 | ○ |
|  |  |  | ○ |
|  |  |  | ○ |
|  |  |  | ○ |
| 23 | 24 | 25 | ○ |
|  |  |  | ○ |
|  |  |  | ○ |
|  |  |  | ○ |
|  |  |  | ○ |
| 30 | 31 |  | NOTES |

# February 2026

| MONDAY | TUESDAY | WEDNESDAY | THURSDAY |
|---|---|---|---|
|  |  |  |  |
| 2 | 3 | 4 | 5 |
| 9 | 10 | 11 | 12 |
| 16 | 17 | 18 | 19 |
| 23 | 24 | 25 | 26 |

# February

| FRIDAY | SATURDAY | SUNDAY | NOTES |
|---|---|---|---|
|  |  | 1 | ○ |
|  |  |  | ○ |
|  |  |  | ○ |
|  |  |  | ○ |
|  |  |  | ○ |
| 6 | 7 | 8 | ○ |
|  |  |  | ○ |
|  |  |  | ○ |
|  |  |  | ○ |
| 13 | 14 | 15 | ○ |
|  |  |  | ○ |
|  |  |  | ○ |
|  |  |  | ○ |
|  |  |  | ○ |
| 20 | 21 | 22 | ○ |
|  |  |  | ○ |
|  |  |  | ○ |
|  |  |  | ○ |
|  |  |  | ○ |
| 27 | 28 |  | NOTES |

# March 2026

| MONDAY | TUESDAY | WEDNESDAY | THURSDAY |
|---|---|---|---|
| | | | |
| 2 | 3 | 4 | 5 |
| 9 | 10 | 11 | 12 |
| 16 | 17 | 18 | 19 |
| 23 | 24 | 25 | 26 |

# March

## 2026

| FRIDAY | SATURDAY | SUNDAY | NOTES |
|---|---|---|---|
| | | 1 | ○ |
| | | | ○ |
| | | | ○ |
| | | | ○ |
| | | | ○ |
| 6 | 7 | 8 | ○ |
| | | | ○ |
| | | | ○ |
| | | | ○ |
| 13 | 14 | 15 | ○ |
| | | | ○ |
| | | | ○ |
| | | | ○ |
| | | | ○ |
| 20 | 21 | 22 | ○ |
| | | | ○ |
| | | | ○ |
| | | | ○ |
| | | | ○ |
| 27 | 28 | 29 | 30 |
| | | | 31 |

# April 2026

| MONDAY | TUESDAY | WEDNESDAY | THURSDAY |
|---|---|---|---|
|  |  | 1 | 2 |
| 6 | 7 | 8 | 9 |
| 13 | 14 | 15 | 16 |
| 20 | 21 | 22 | 23 |
| 27 | 28 | 29 | 30 |

# April

| FRIDAY | SATURDAY | SUNDAY | NOTES |
|---|---|---|---|
| 3 | 4 | 5 | ○ |
| | | | ○ |
| | | | ○ |
| | | | ○ |
| | | | ○ |
| 10 | 11 | 12 | ○ |
| | | | ○ |
| | | | ○ |
| | | | ○ |
| 17 | 18 | 19 | ○ |
| | | | ○ |
| | | | ○ |
| | | | ○ |
| | | | ○ |
| 24 | 25 | 26 | ○ |
| | | | ○ |
| | | | ○ |
| | | | ○ |
| | | | ○ |
| | | | NOTES |

# May
## 2026

| MONDAY | TUESDAY | WEDNESDAY | THURSDAY |
|---|---|---|---|
|  |  |  |  |
| 4 | 5 | 6 | 7 |
| 11 | 12 | 13 | 14 |
| 18 | 19 | 20 | 21 |
| 25 | 26 | 27 | 28 |

# May

| FRIDAY | SATURDAY | SUNDAY | NOTES |
|---|---|---|---|
| 1 | 2 | 3 | ○ |
|  |  |  | ○ |
|  |  |  | ○ |
|  |  |  | ○ |
|  |  |  | ○ |
| 8 | 9 | 10 | ○ |
|  |  |  | ○ |
|  |  |  | ○ |
|  |  |  | ○ |
|  |  |  | ○ |
| 15 | 16 | 17 | ○ |
|  |  |  | ○ |
|  |  |  | ○ |
|  |  |  | ○ |
|  |  |  | ○ |
| 22 | 23 | 24 | ○ |
|  |  |  | ○ |
|  |  |  | ○ |
|  |  |  | ○ |
|  |  |  | ○ |
| 29 | 30 | 31 | Notes |

# June
## 2026

| MONDAY | TUESDAY | WEDNESDAY | THURSDAY |
|---|---|---|---|
| 1 | 2 | 3 | 4 |
| 8 | 9 | 10 | 11 |
| 15 | 16 | 17 | 18 |
| 22 | 23 | 24 | 25 |
| 29 | 30 | | |

# June

## 2026

| FRIDAY | SATURDAY | SUNDAY | NOTES |
|---|---|---|---|
| 5 | 6 | 7 | ○ |
| | | | ○ |
| | | | ○ |
| | | | ○ |
| | | | ○ |
| 12 | 13 | 14 | ○ |
| | | | ○ |
| | | | ○ |
| | | | ○ |
| 19 | 20 | 21 | ○ |
| | | | ○ |
| | | | ○ |
| | | | ○ |
| | | | ○ |
| 26 | 27 | 28 | ○ |
| | | | ○ |
| | | | ○ |
| | | | ○ |
| | | | ○ |
| | | | Notes |

# July

| MONDAY | TUESDAY | WEDNESDAY | THURSDAY |
|---|---|---|---|
| | | 1 | 2 |
| 6 | 7 | 8 | 9 |
| 13 | 14 | 15 | 16 |
| 20 | 21 | 22 | 23 |
| 27 | 28 | 29 | 30 |

# July

2026

| FRIDAY | SATURDAY | SUNDAY | NOTES |
|---|---|---|---|
| 3 | 4 | 5 | ○ |
| | | | ○ |
| | | | ○ |
| | | | ○ |
| | | | ○ |
| 10 | 11 | 12 | ○ |
| | | | ○ |
| | | | ○ |
| | | | ○ |
| 17 | 18 | 19 | ○ |
| | | | ○ |
| | | | ○ |
| | | | ○ |
| | | | ○ |
| 24 | 25 | 26 | ○ |
| | | | ○ |
| | | | ○ |
| | | | ○ |
| | | | ○ |
| 31 | | | NOTES |

# August 2026

| MONDAY | TUESDAY | WEDNESDAY | THURSDAY |
|---|---|---|---|
|  |  |  |  |
| 3 | 4 | 5 | 6 |
| 10 | 11 | 12 | 13 |
| 17 | 18 | 19 | 20 |
| 24 | 25 | 26 | 27 |

# August

| FRIDAY | SATURDAY | SUNDAY | NOTES |
|--------|----------|--------|-------|
|  | 1 | 2 | ○ |
|  |  |  | ○ |
|  |  |  | ○ |
|  |  |  | ○ |
|  |  |  | ○ |
| 7 | 8 | 9 | ○ |
|  |  |  | ○ |
|  |  |  | ○ |
|  |  |  | ○ |
| 14 | 15 | 16 | ○ |
|  |  |  | ○ |
|  |  |  | ○ |
|  |  |  | ○ |
|  |  |  | ○ |
| 21 | 22 | 23 | ○ |
|  |  |  | ○ |
|  |  |  | ○ |
|  |  |  | ○ |
|  |  |  | ○ |
| 28 | 29 | 30 | 31 |

# September 2026

| MONDAY | TUESDAY | WEDNESDAY | THURSDAY |
|---|---|---|---|
| | 1 | 2 | 3 |
| 7 | 8 | 9 | 10 |
| 14 | 15 | 16 | 17 |
| 21 | 22 | 23 | 24 |
| 28 | 29 | 30 | |

# September

| FRIDAY | SATURDAY | SUNDAY | NOTES |
|---|---|---|---|
| 4 | 5 | 6 | ○ |
| | | | ○ |
| | | | ○ |
| | | | ○ |
| | | | ○ |
| 11 | 12 | 13 | ○ |
| | | | ○ |
| | | | ○ |
| | | | ○ |
| 18 | 19 | 20 | ○ |
| | | | ○ |
| | | | ○ |
| | | | ○ |
| | | | ○ |
| 25 | 26 | 27 | ○ |
| | | | ○ |
| | | | ○ |
| | | | ○ |
| | | | ○ |
| | | | NOTES |

# October 2026

| MONDAY | TUESDAY | WEDNESDAY | THURSDAY |
|---|---|---|---|
| | | | 1 |
| 5 | 6 | 7 | 8 |
| 12 | 13 | 14 | 15 |
| 19 | 20 | 21 | 22 |
| 26 | 27 | 28 | 29 |

# October 2026

| FRIDAY | SATURDAY | SUNDAY | NOTES |
|---|---|---|---|
| 2 | 3 | 4 | ○ |
|  |  |  | ○ |
|  |  |  | ○ |
|  |  |  | ○ |
|  |  |  | ○ |
| 9 | 10 | 11 | ○ |
|  |  |  | ○ |
|  |  |  | ○ |
|  |  |  | ○ |
| 16 | 17 | 18 | ○ |
|  |  |  | ○ |
|  |  |  | ○ |
|  |  |  | ○ |
|  |  |  | ○ |
| 23 | 24 | 25 | ○ |
|  |  |  | ○ |
|  |  |  | ○ |
|  |  |  | ○ |
|  |  |  | ○ |
| 30 | 31 |  | NOTES |

# November

| MONDAY | TUESDAY | WEDNESDAY | THURSDAY |
|---|---|---|---|
|  |  |  |  |
| 2 | 3 | 4 | 5 |
| 9 | 10 | 11 | 12 |
| 16 | 17 | 18 | 19 |
| 23 | 24 | 25 | 26 |

# November

| FRIDAY | SATURDAY | SUNDAY | NOTES |
|---|---|---|---|
| | | 1 | ○ |
| | | | ○ |
| | | | ○ |
| | | | ○ |
| | | | ○ |
| 6 | 7 | 8 | ○ |
| | | | ○ |
| | | | ○ |
| | | | ○ |
| 13 | 14 | 15 | ○ |
| | | | ○ |
| | | | ○ |
| | | | ○ |
| | | | ○ |
| 20 | 21 | 22 | ○ |
| | | | ○ |
| | | | ○ |
| | | | ○ |
| | | | ○ |
| 27 | 28 | 29 | 30 |

# December 2026

| MONDAY | TUESDAY | WEDNESDAY | THURSDAY |
|---|---|---|---|
| | 1 | 2 | 3 |
| 7 | 8 | 9 | 10 |
| 14 | 15 | 16 | 17 |
| 21 | 22 | 23 | 24 |
| 28 | 29 | 30 | 31 |

# December 2026

| FRIDAY | SATURDAY | SUNDAY | NOTES |
|---|---|---|---|
| 4 | 5 | 6 | ○ |
|  |  |  | ○ |
|  |  |  | ○ |
|  |  |  | ○ |
|  |  |  | ○ |
| 11 | 12 | 13 | ○ |
|  |  |  | ○ |
|  |  |  | ○ |
|  |  |  | ○ |
| 18 | 19 | 20 | ○ |
|  |  |  | ○ |
|  |  |  | ○ |
|  |  |  | ○ |
|  |  |  | ○ |
| 25 | 26 | 27 | ○ |
|  |  |  | ○ |
|  |  |  | ○ |
|  |  |  | ○ |
|  |  |  | ○ |
|  |  |  | NOTES |

# December
## 2025

**01** MONDAY
- ○ _____
- ○ _____
- ○ _____
- ○ _____
- ○ _____
- ○ _____
- ○ _____
- ○ _____

**02** TUESDAY
- ○ _____
- ○ _____
- ○ _____
- ○ _____
- ○ _____
- ○ _____
- ○ _____
- ○ _____

**03** WEDNESDAY
- ○ _____
- ○ _____
- ○ _____
- ○ _____
- ○ _____
- ○ _____
- ○ _____
- ○ _____

**04** FRIDAY
- ○ _____
- ○ _____
- ○ _____
- ○ _____
- ○ _____

**05** FRIDAY

○
○
○
○
○
○
○
○

**06** SATURDAY

○
○
○
○
○
○
○
○

**07** SUNDAY

○
○
○
○
○
○
○
○

**08** MONDAY

○
○
○
○
○

**09** TUESDAY

○ _____
○ _____
○ _____
○ _____
○ _____
○ _____
○ _____
○ _____

**10** WEDNESDAY

○ _____
○ _____
○ _____
○ _____
○ _____
○ _____
○ _____
○ _____

**11** THURSDAY

○ _____
○ _____
○ _____
○ _____
○ _____
○ _____
○ _____
○ _____

**12** FRIDAY

○ _____
○ _____
○ _____
○ _____
○ _____

**13** SATURDAY

**14** SUNDAY

**15** MONDAY

**16** TUESDAY

**17** WEDNESDAY

○ _____
○ _____
○ _____
○ _____
○ _____
○ _____
○ _____
○ _____

**18** THURSDAY

○ _____
○ _____
○ _____
○ _____
○ _____
○ _____
○ _____
○ _____

**19** FRIDAY

○ _____
○ _____
○ _____
○ _____
○ _____
○ _____
○ _____
○ _____

**20** SATURDAY

○ _____
○ _____
○ _____
○ _____
○ _____

**21** SUNDAY

**22** MONDAY

**23** TUESDAY

**24** WEDNESDAY

# December
## 2025

**25** THURSDAY

○ _____
○ _____
○ _____
○ _____
○ _____
○ _____
○ _____
○ _____

**26** FRIDAY

○ _____
○ _____
○ _____
○ _____
○ _____
○ _____
○ _____
○ _____

**27** SATURDAY

○ _____
○ _____
○ _____
○ _____
○ _____
○ _____
○ _____
○ _____

**28** SUNDAY

○ _____
○ _____
○ _____
○ _____
○ _____

**29** MONDAY

○
○
○
○
○
○
○
○

**30** TUESDAY

○
○
○
○
○
○
○
○

**31** WEDNESDAY

○
○
○
○
○
○
○
○

NOTES

# January
## 2026

**01** THURSDAY
○
○
○
○
○
○
○
○

**02** FRIDAY
○
○
○
○
○
○
○
○

**03** SATURDAY
○
○
○
○
○
○
○
○

**04** SUNDAY
○
○
○
○
○

**05** MONDAY

○
○
○
○
○
○
○
○

**06** TUESDAY

○
○
○
○
○
○
○
○

**07** WEDNESDAY

○
○
○
○
○
○
○
○

**08** THURSDAY

○
○
○
○
○

**09** FRIDAY
○
○
○
○
○
○
○
○

**10** SATURDAY
○
○
○
○
○
○
○
○

**11** SUNDAY
○
○
○
○
○
○
○
○

**12** MONDAY
○
○
○
○
○

**13** TUESDAY

○
○
○
○
○
○
○
○

**14** WEDNESDAY

○
○
○
○
○
○
○
○
○

**15** THURSDAY

○
○
○
○
○
○
○
○

**16** FRIDAY

○
○
○
○
○

**17** SATURDAY

○
○
○
○
○
○
○
○

**18** SUNDAY

○
○
○
○
○
○
○
○

**19** MONDAY

○
○
○
○
○
○
○
○

**20** TUESDAY

○
○
○
○
○

# January
## 2026

**21** WEDNESDAY
- ○
- ○
- ○
- ○
- ○
- ○
- ○
- ○

**22** THURSDAY
- ○
- ○
- ○
- ○
- ○
- ○
- ○
- ○

**23** FRIDAY
- ○
- ○
- ○
- ○
- ○
- ○
- ○
- ○

**24** SATURDAY
- ○
- ○
- ○
- ○
- ○

**25** SUNDAY

○
○
○
○
○
○
○
○

**26** MONDAY

○
○
○
○
○
○
○
○

**27** TUESDAY

○
○
○
○
○
○
○
○

**28** WEDNESDAY

○
○
○
○
○

**29** THURSDAY

○
○
○
○
○
○
○
○

**30** FRIDAY

○
○
○
○
○
○
○
○

**31** SATURDAY

○
○
○
○
○
○
○
○

NOTES

# February
## 2026

**01** SUNDAY
- ○ _____
- ○ _____
- ○ _____
- ○ _____
- ○ _____
- ○ _____
- ○ _____
- ○ _____

**02** MONDAY
- ○ _____
- ○ _____
- ○ _____
- ○ _____
- ○ _____
- ○ _____
- ○ _____
- ○ _____

**03** TUESDAY
- ○ _____
- ○ _____
- ○ _____
- ○ _____
- ○ _____
- ○ _____
- ○ _____
- ○ _____

**04** WEDNESDAY
- ○ _____
- ○ _____
- ○ _____
- ○ _____
- ○ _____

# February
## 2026

**05** THURSDAY
○
○
○
○
○
○
○
○

**06** FRIDAY
○
○
○
○
○
○
○
○

**07** SATURDAY
○
○
○
○
○
○
○
○

**08** SUNDAY
○
○
○
○
○

# February 2026

**09** MONDAY

○
○
○
○
○
○
○
○

**10** TUESDAY

○
○
○
○
○
○
○
○

**11** WEDNESDAY

○
○
○
○
○
○
○
○

**12** THURSDAY

○
○
○
○
○

# February
## 2026

**13** FRIDAY

○
○
○
○
○
○
○
○

**14** SATURDAY

○
○
○
○
○
○
○
○

**15** SUNDAY

○
○
○
○
○
○
○
○

**16** MONDAY

○
○
○
○
○

*February*
2026

**17** TUESDAY

○
○
○
○
○
○
○
○

**18** WEDNESDAY

○
○
○
○
○
○
○
○

**19** THURSDAY

○
○
○
○
○
○
○
○

**20** FRIDAY

○
○
○
○
○

**21** SATURDAY

○
○
○
○
○
○
○
○

**22** SUNDAY

○
○
○
○
○
○
○
○

**23** MONDAY

○
○
○
○
○
○
○
○

**24** TUESDAY

○
○
○
○
○

*February*
2026

**25** WEDNESDAY

○
○
○
○
○
○
○
○

**26** THURSDAY

○
○
○
○
○
○
○
○

**27** FRIDAY

○
○
○
○
○
○
○
○

**28** SATURDAY

○
○
○
○
○

# *March* 2026

**01** SUNDAY

○
○
○
○
○
○
○
○

**02** MONDAY

○
○
○
○
○
○
○
○
○

**03** TUESDAY

○
○
○
○
○
○
○
○

**04** WEDNESDAY

○
○
○
○
○

**05** THURSDAY

○ _____
○ _____
○ _____
○ _____
○ _____
○ _____
○ _____
○ _____

**06** FRIDAY

○ _____
○ _____
○ _____
○ _____
○ _____
○ _____
○ _____
○ _____

**07** SATURDAY

○ _____
○ _____
○ _____
○ _____
○ _____
○ _____
○ _____
○ _____

**08** SUNDAY

○ _____
○ _____
○ _____
○ _____
○ _____

**09** MONDAY

○
○
○
○
○
○
○
○

**10** TUESDAY

○
○
○
○
○
○
○
○

**11** WEDNESDAY

○
○
○
○
○
○
○
○

**12** THURSDAY

○
○
○
○
○

**13** FRIDAY

○ _____
○ _____
○ _____
○ _____
○ _____
○ _____
○ _____
○ _____

**14** SATURDAY

○ _____
○ _____
○ _____
○ _____
○ _____
○ _____
○ _____
○ _____

**15** SUNDAY

○ _____
○ _____
○ _____
○ _____
○ _____
○ _____
○ _____
○ _____

**16** MONDAY

○ _____
○ _____
○ _____
○ _____
○ _____

**17** TUESDAY

○
○
○
○
○
○
○
○

**18** WEDNESDAY

○
○
○
○
○
○
○
○
○

**19** THURSDAY

○
○
○
○
○
○
○
○

**20** FRIDAY

○
○
○
○
○

# March
## 2026

**21** SATURDAY

○
○
○
○
○
○
○
○

**22** SUNDAY

○
○
○
○
○
○
○
○

**23** MONDAY

○
○
○
○
○
○
○
○

**24** TUESDAY

○
○
○
○
○

**25** WEDNESDAY

○
○
○
○
○
○
○
○

**26** THURSDAY

○
○
○
○
○
○
○
○

**27** FRIDAY

○
○
○
○
○
○
○
○

**28** SATURDAY

○
○
○
○
○

**29** SUNDAY

○ _____
○ _____
○ _____
○ _____
○ _____
○ _____
○ _____
○ _____

**30** MONDAY

○ _____
○ _____
○ _____
○ _____
○ _____
○ _____
○ _____
○ _____

**31** TUESDAY

○ _____
○ _____
○ _____
○ _____
○ _____
○ _____
○ _____
○ _____

NOTES

_____
_____
_____
_____

# April
## 2026

**01** WEDNESDAY
- ○
- ○
- ○
- ○
- ○
- ○
- ○
- ○

**02** THURSDAY
- ○
- ○
- ○
- ○
- ○
- ○
- ○
- ○

**03** FRIDAY
- ○
- ○
- ○
- ○
- ○
- ○
- ○
- ○

**04** SATURDAY
- ○
- ○
- ○
- ○
- ○

# April
## 2026

**05** SUNDAY

- ○
- ○
- ○
- ○
- ○
- ○
- ○
- ○

**06** MONDAY

- ○
- ○
- ○
- ○
- ○
- ○
- ○
- ○

**07** TUESDAY

- ○
- ○
- ○
- ○
- ○
- ○
- ○
- ○

**08** WEDNESDAY

- ○
- ○
- ○
- ○
- ○

**09** THURSDAY

○
○
○
○
○
○
○
○

**10** FRIDAY

○
○
○
○
○
○
○
○

**11** SATURDAY

○
○
○
○
○
○
○
○

**12** SUNDAY

○
○
○
○
○

**13** MONDAY

○ _____
○ _____
○ _____
○ _____
○ _____
○ _____
○ _____
○ _____

**14** TUESDAY

○ _____
○ _____
○ _____
○ _____
○ _____
○ _____
○ _____
○ _____

**15** WEDNESDAY

○ _____
○ _____
○ _____
○ _____
○ _____
○ _____
○ _____
○ _____

**16** THURSDAY

○ _____
○ _____
○ _____
○ _____
○ _____

# April
## 2026

**17** FRIDAY

○
○
○
○
○
○
○
○

**18** SATURDAY

○
○
○
○
○
○
○
○

**19** SUNDAY

○
○
○
○
○
○
○
○

**20** MONDAY

○
○
○
○
○

**21** TUESDAY

○ _____
○ _____
○ _____
○ _____
○ _____
○ _____
○ _____
○ _____

**22** WEDNESDAY

○ _____
○ _____
○ _____
○ _____
○ _____
○ _____
○ _____
○ _____

**23** THURSDAY

○ _____
○ _____
○ _____
○ _____
○ _____
○ _____
○ _____
○ _____

**24** FRIDAY

○ _____
○ _____
○ _____
○ _____
○ _____

**25** SATURDAY

**26** SUNDAY

**27** MONDAY

**28** TUESDAY

**29** WEDNESDAY

○ _____
○ _____
○ _____
○ _____
○ _____
○ _____
○ _____
○ _____

**30** THURSDAY

○ _____
○ _____
○ _____
○ _____
○ _____
○ _____
○ _____
○ _____

NOTES

_____
_____
_____
_____
_____
_____
_____
_____
_____
_____
_____
_____

# May
## 2026

**01** FRIDAY

○ _____
○ _____
○ _____
○ _____
○ _____
○ _____
○ _____
○ _____

**02** SATURDAY

○ _____
○ _____
○ _____
○ _____
○ _____
○ _____
○ _____
○ _____

**03** SUNDAY

○ _____
○ _____
○ _____
○ _____
○ _____
○ _____
○ _____
○ _____

**04** MONDAY

○ _____
○ _____
○ _____
○ _____
○ _____

# May
## 2026

**05** TUESDAY
- ○
- ○
- ○
- ○
- ○
- ○
- ○
- ○

**06** WEDNESDAY
- ○
- ○
- ○
- ○
- ○
- ○
- ○
- ○

**07** THURSDAY
- ○
- ○
- ○
- ○
- ○
- ○
- ○
- ○

**08** FRIDAY
- ○
- ○
- ○
- ○
- ○

# *May*
## 2026

**09** SATURDAY
- ○
- ○
- ○
- ○
- ○
- ○
- ○
- ○

**10** SUNDAY
- ○
- ○
- ○
- ○
- ○
- ○
- ○
- ○

**11** MONDAY
- ○
- ○
- ○
- ○
- ○
- ○
- ○
- ○

**12** TUESDAY
- ○
- ○
- ○
- ○
- ○

**13** WEDNESDAY

○
○
○
○
○
○
○
○

**14** THURSDAY

○
○
○
○
○
○
○
○

**15** FRIDAY

○
○
○
○
○
○
○
○

**16** SATURDAY

○
○
○
○
○

**17** SUNDAY

○
○
○
○
○
○
○
○

**18** MONDAY

○
○
○
○
○
○
○
○

**19** TUESDAY

○
○
○
○
○
○
○
○

**20** WEDNESDAY

○
○
○
○
○

# May
## 2026

**21** THURSDAY
○
○
○
○
○
○
○
○

**22** FRIDAY
○
○
○
○
○
○
○
○

**23** SATURDAY
○
○
○
○
○
○
○
○

**24** SUNDAY
○
○
○
○
○

**25** MONDAY

○
○
○
○
○
○
○
○

**26** TUESDAY

○
○
○
○
○
○
○
○

**27** WEDNESDAY

○
○
○
○
○
○
○
○

**28** THURSDAY

○
○
○
○
○

**29** FRIDAY

○ _____
○ _____
○ _____
○ _____
○ _____
○ _____
○ _____
○ _____

**30** SATURDAY

○ _____
○ _____
○ _____
○ _____
○ _____
○ _____
○ _____
○ _____

**31** SUNDAY

○ _____
○ _____
○ _____
○ _____
○ _____
○ _____
○ _____
○ _____

NOTES

_____
_____
_____
_____
_____

# June 2026

**01** MONDAY

○
○
○
○
○
○
○
○

**02** TUESDAY

○
○
○
○
○
○
○
○

**03** WEDNESDAY

○
○
○
○
○
○
○
○

**04** THURSDAY

○
○
○
○
○

# June
## 2026

**05** FRIDAY

○ _____
○ _____
○ _____
○ _____
○ _____
○ _____
○ _____
○ _____

**06** SATURDAY

○ _____
○ _____
○ _____
○ _____
○ _____
○ _____
○ _____
○ _____

**07** SUNDAY

○ _____
○ _____
○ _____
○ _____
○ _____
○ _____
○ _____
○ _____

**08** MONDAY

○ _____
○ _____
○ _____
○ _____
○ _____

**09** TUESDAY

○
○
○
○
○
○
○
○

**10** WEDNESDAY

○
○
○
○
○
○
○
○

**11** THURSDAY

○
○
○
○
○
○
○
○

**12** FRIDAY

○
○
○
○
○

## 13 SATURDAY

○ _____
○ _____
○ _____
○ _____
○ _____
○ _____
○ _____
○ _____

## 14 SUNDAY

○ _____
○ _____
○ _____
○ _____
○ _____
○ _____
○ _____
○ _____

## 15 MONDAY

○ _____
○ _____
○ _____
○ _____
○ _____
○ _____
○ _____
○ _____

## 16 TUESDAY

○ _____
○ _____
○ _____
○ _____
○ _____

**17** WEDNESDAY

○
○
○
○
○
○
○
○

**18** THURSDAY

○
○
○
○
○
○
○
○

**19** FRIDAY

○
○
○
○
○
○
○
○

**20** SATURDAY

○
○
○
○
○

**21** SUNDAY

○ _____
○ _____
○ _____
○ _____
○ _____
○ _____
○ _____
○ _____

**22** MONDAY

○ _____
○ _____
○ _____
○ _____
○ _____
○ _____
○ _____
○ _____

**23** TUESDAY

○ _____
○ _____
○ _____
○ _____
○ _____
○ _____
○ _____
○ _____

**24** WEDNESDAY

○ _____
○ _____
○ _____
○ _____
○ _____

# June 2026

## 25 THURSDAY

○
○
○
○
○
○
○
○

## 26 FRIDAY

○
○
○
○
○
○
○
○

## 27 SATURDAY

○
○
○
○
○
○
○
○

## 28 SUNDAY

○
○
○
○
○

# June
## 2026

**29** MONDAY

○ _____
○ _____
○ _____
○ _____
○ _____
○ _____
○ _____
○ _____

**30** TUESDAY

○ _____
○ _____
○ _____
○ _____
○ _____
○ _____
○ _____
○ _____

NOTES

**01** WEDNESDAY

○
○
○
○
○
○
○
○

**02** THURSDAY

○
○
○
○
○
○
○
○

**03** FRIDAY

○
○
○
○
○
○
○
○

**04** SATURDAY

○
○
○
○
○

# July
## 2026

**05** SUNDAY
○ _____
○ _____
○ _____
○ _____
○ _____
○ _____
○ _____
○ _____

**06** MONDAY
○ _____
○ _____
○ _____
○ _____
○ _____
○ _____
○ _____
○ _____

**07** TUESDAY
○ _____
○ _____
○ _____
○ _____
○ _____
○ _____
○ _____
○ _____

**08** WEDNESDAY
○ _____
○ _____
○ _____
○ _____
○ _____

# July
## 2026

**09** THURSDAY

○
○
○
○
○
○
○
○

**10** FRIDAY

○
○
○
○
○
○
○
○

**11** SATURDAY

○
○
○
○
○
○
○
○

**12** SUNDAY

○
○
○
○
○

**13** MONDAY

○
○
○
○
○
○
○
○

**14** TUESDAY

○
○
○
○
○
○
○
○

**15** WEDNESDAY

○
○
○
○
○
○
○
○

**16** THURSDAY

○
○
○
○
○

**17** FRIDAY

○
○
○
○
○
○
○
○

**18** SATURDAY

○
○
○
○
○
○
○
○

**19** SUNDAY

○
○
○
○
○
○
○
○

**20** MONDAY

○
○
○
○
○

# July
## 2026

**21** TUESDAY

○ _____
○ _____
○ _____
○ _____
○ _____
○ _____
○ _____
○ _____

**22** WEDNESDAY

○ _____
○ _____
○ _____
○ _____
○ _____
○ _____
○ _____
○ _____

**23** THURSDAY

○ _____
○ _____
○ _____
○ _____
○ _____
○ _____
○ _____
○ _____

**24** FRIDAY

○ _____
○ _____
○ _____
○ _____
○ _____

**25** SATURDAY

○ _____
○ _____
○ _____
○ _____
○ _____
○ _____
○ _____
○ _____

**26** SUNDAY

○ _____
○ _____
○ _____
○ _____
○ _____
○ _____
○ _____
○ _____

**27** MONDAY

○ _____
○ _____
○ _____
○ _____
○ _____
○ _____
○ _____
○ _____

**28** TUESDAY

○ _____
○ _____
○ _____
○ _____
○ _____

# July
## 2026

**29** WEDNESDAY

- ○
- ○
- ○
- ○
- ○
- ○
- ○
- ○

**30** THURSDAY

- ○
- ○
- ○
- ○
- ○
- ○
- ○
- ○

**31** FRIDAY

- ○
- ○
- ○
- ○
- ○
- ○
- ○
- ○

NOTES

# August
## 2026

**01** SATURDAY

- ○ _____
- ○ _____
- ○ _____
- ○ _____
- ○ _____
- ○ _____
- ○ _____
- ○ _____

**02** SUNDAY

- ○ _____
- ○ _____
- ○ _____
- ○ _____
- ○ _____
- ○ _____
- ○ _____
- ○ _____

**03** MONDAY

- ○ _____
- ○ _____
- ○ _____
- ○ _____
- ○ _____
- ○ _____
- ○ _____
- ○ _____

**04** TUESDAY

- ○ _____
- ○ _____
- ○ _____
- ○ _____
- ○ _____

**05** WEDNESDAY

○ _____
○ _____
○ _____
○ _____
○ _____
○ _____
○ _____
○ _____

**06** THURSDAY

○ _____
○ _____
○ _____
○ _____
○ _____
○ _____
○ _____
○ _____

**07** FRIDAY

○ _____
○ _____
○ _____
○ _____
○ _____
○ _____
○ _____
○ _____

**08** SATURDAY

○ _____
○ _____
○ _____
○ _____
○ _____

# August
## 2026

**09** SUNDAY
○
○
○
○
○
○
○
○

**10** MONDAY
○
○
○
○
○
○
○
○

**11** TUESDAY
○
○
○
○
○
○
○
○

**12** WEDNESDAY
○
○
○
○
○

**13** THURSDAY

○
○
○
○
○
○
○
○

**14** FRIDAY

○
○
○
○
○
○
○
○

**15** SATURDAY

○
○
○
○
○
○
○
○

**16** SUNDAY

○
○
○
○
○

**17** MONDAY

○
○
○
○
○
○
○
○

**18** TUESDAY

○
○
○
○
○
○
○
○

**19** WEDNESDAY

○
○
○
○
○
○
○
○

**20** THURSDAY

○
○
○
○
○

**21** FRIDAY

○
○
○
○
○
○
○
○

**22** SATURDAY

○
○
○
○
○
○
○
○

**23** SUNDAY

○
○
○
○
○
○
○
○

**24** MONDAY

○
○
○
○
○

# August
## 2026

**25** TUESDAY

○
○
○
○
○
○
○
○

**26** WEDNESDAY

○
○
○
○
○
○
○
○

**27** THURSDAY

○
○
○
○
○
○
○
○

**28** FRIDAY

○
○
○
○
○

**29** SATURDAY

○ _____
○ _____
○ _____
○ _____
○ _____
○ _____
○ _____
○ _____

**30** SUNDAY

○ _____
○ _____
○ _____
○ _____
○ _____
○ _____
○ _____
○ _____

**31** MONDAY

○ _____
○ _____
○ _____
○ _____
○ _____
○ _____
○ _____
○ _____

NOTES

_____
_____
_____
_____
_____

**01** TUESDAY

○ _____
○ _____
○ _____
○ _____
○ _____
○ _____
○ _____
○ _____

**02** WEDNESDAY

○ _____
○ _____
○ _____
○ _____
○ _____
○ _____
○ _____
○ _____

**03** THURSDAY

○ _____
○ _____
○ _____
○ _____
○ _____
○ _____
○ _____
○ _____

**04** FRIDAY

○ _____
○ _____
○ _____
○ _____
○ _____

**05** SATURDAY

○ _____
○ _____
○ _____
○ _____
○ _____
○ _____
○ _____
○ _____

**06** SUNDAY

○ _____
○ _____
○ _____
○ _____
○ _____
○ _____
○ _____
○ _____

**07** MONDAY

○ _____
○ _____
○ _____
○ _____
○ _____
○ _____
○ _____
○ _____

**08** TUESDAY

○ _____
○ _____
○ _____
○ _____
○ _____

**09** WEDNESDAY

○ _____
○ _____
○ _____
○ _____
○ _____
○ _____
○ _____
○ _____

**10** THURSDAY

○ _____
○ _____
○ _____
○ _____
○ _____
○ _____
○ _____
○ _____

**11** FRIDAY

○ _____
○ _____
○ _____
○ _____
○ _____
○ _____
○ _____
○ _____

**12** SATURDAY

○ _____
○ _____
○ _____
○ _____
○ _____

**13** SUNDAY

○
○
○
○
○
○
○
○

**14** MONDAY

○
○
○
○
○
○
○
○

**15** TUESDAY

○
○
○
○
○
○
○
○

**16** WEDNESDAY

○
○
○
○
○

**17** THURSDAY

○
○
○
○
○
○
○
○

**18** FRIDAY

○
○
○
○
○
○
○
○

**19** SATURDAY

○
○
○
○
○
○
○
○

**20** SUNDAY

○
○
○
○
○

# September
## 2026

**21** MONDAY
- ○ _____
- ○ _____
- ○ _____
- ○ _____
- ○ _____
- ○ _____
- ○ _____
- ○ _____

**22** TUESDAY
- ○ _____
- ○ _____
- ○ _____
- ○ _____
- ○ _____
- ○ _____
- ○ _____
- ○ _____

**23** WEDNESDAY
- ○ _____
- ○ _____
- ○ _____
- ○ _____
- ○ _____
- ○ _____
- ○ _____
- ○ _____

**24** THURSDAY
- ○ _____
- ○ _____
- ○ _____
- ○ _____
- ○ _____

## 25 FRIDAY

○
○
○
○
○
○
○
○

## 26 SATURDAY

○
○
○
○
○
○
○
○

## 27 SUNDAY

○
○
○
○
○
○
○
○

## 28 MONDAY

○
○
○
○
○

**29** TUESDAY

- ○
- ○
- ○
- ○
- ○
- ○
- ○
- ○

**30** WEDNESDAY

- ○
- ○
- ○
- ○
- ○
- ○
- ○
- ○

NOTES

# October
## 2026

**01** THURSDAY
○
○
○
○
○
○
○
○

**02** FRIDAY
○
○
○
○
○
○
○
○

**03** SATURDAY
○
○
○
○
○
○
○
○

**04** SUNDAY
○
○
○
○
○

# October
## 2026

**05** MONDAY

○ _____
○ _____
○ _____
○ _____
○ _____
○ _____
○ _____
○ _____

**06** TUESDAY

○ _____
○ _____
○ _____
○ _____
○ _____
○ _____
○ _____
○ _____

**07** WEDNESDAY

○ _____
○ _____
○ _____
○ _____
○ _____
○ _____
○ _____
○ _____

**08** THURSDAY

○ _____
○ _____
○ _____
○ _____
○ _____

**09** FRIDAY

○
○
○
○
○
○
○
○

**10** SATURDAY

○
○
○
○
○
○
○
○

**11** SUNDAY

○
○
○
○
○
○
○
○

**12** MONDAY

○
○
○
○
○

**13** TUESDAY

○ _____
○ _____
○ _____
○ _____
○ _____
○ _____
○ _____
○ _____

**14** WEDNESDAY

○ _____
○ _____
○ _____
○ _____
○ _____
○ _____
○ _____
○ _____

**15** THURSDAY

○ _____
○ _____
○ _____
○ _____
○ _____
○ _____
○ _____
○ _____

**16** FRIDAY

○ _____
○ _____
○ _____
○ _____
○ _____

# October
## 2026

**17** SATURDAY
○
○
○
○
○
○
○
○

**18** SUNDAY
○
○
○
○
○
○
○
○

**19** MONDAY
○
○
○
○
○
○
○
○

**20** TUESDAY
○
○
○
○
○

**21** WEDNESDAY

○ _____
○ _____
○ _____
○ _____
○ _____
○ _____
○ _____
○ _____

**22** THURSDAY

○ _____
○ _____
○ _____
○ _____
○ _____
○ _____
○ _____
○ _____

**23** FRIDAY

○ _____
○ _____
○ _____
○ _____
○ _____
○ _____
○ _____
○ _____

**24** SATURDAY

○ _____
○ _____
○ _____
○ _____
○ _____

**25** SUNDAY

**26** MONDAY

**27** TUESDAY

**28** WEDNESDAY

# October
## 2026

**29** THURSDAY

○
○
○
○
○
○
○
○

**30** FRIDAY

○
○
○
○
○
○
○
○

**31** SATURDAY

○
○
○
○
○
○
○
○

NOTES

# November
## 2026

**01** SUNDAY
- ○
- ○
- ○
- ○
- ○
- ○
- ○
- ○

**02** MONDAY
- ○
- ○
- ○
- ○
- ○
- ○
- ○
- ○

**03** TUESDAY
- ○
- ○
- ○
- ○
- ○
- ○
- ○
- ○

**04** WEDNESDAY
- ○
- ○
- ○
- ○
- ○

**05** THURSDAY

○ _____
○ _____
○ _____
○ _____
○ _____
○ _____
○ _____
○ _____

**06** FRIDAY

○ _____
○ _____
○ _____
○ _____
○ _____
○ _____
○ _____
○ _____

**07** SATURDAY

○ _____
○ _____
○ _____
○ _____
○ _____
○ _____
○ _____
○ _____

**08** SUNDAY

○ _____
○ _____
○ _____
○ _____
○ _____

# November
## 2026

**09** MONDAY

○ _____
○ _____
○ _____
○ _____
○ _____
○ _____
○ _____
○ _____

**10** TUESDAY

○ _____
○ _____
○ _____
○ _____
○ _____
○ _____
○ _____
○ _____

**11** WEDNESDAY

○ _____
○ _____
○ _____
○ _____
○ _____
○ _____
○ _____
○ _____

**12** THURSDAY

○ _____
○ _____
○ _____
○ _____
○ _____

**13** FRIDAY

○ _____
○ _____
○ _____
○ _____
○ _____
○ _____
○ _____
○ _____

**14** SATURDAY

○ _____
○ _____
○ _____
○ _____
○ _____
○ _____
○ _____
○ _____

**15** SUNDAY

○ _____
○ _____
○ _____
○ _____
○ _____
○ _____
○ _____
○ _____

**16** MONDAY

○ _____
○ _____
○ _____
○ _____
○ _____

**17** TUESDAY

○
○
○
○
○
○
○
○

**18** WEDNESDAY

○
○
○
○
○
○
○
○

**19** THURSDAY

○
○
○
○
○
○
○
○

**20** FRIDAY

○
○
○
○
○

**21** SATURDAY

○
○
○
○
○
○
○
○

**22** SUNDAY

○
○
○
○
○
○
○
○

**23** MONDAY

○
○
○
○
○
○
○
○

**24** TUESDAY

○
○
○
○
○

# November
## 2026

**25** WEDNESDAY

○ _____
○ _____
○ _____
○ _____
○ _____
○ _____
○ _____
○ _____

**26** THURSDAY

○ _____
○ _____
○ _____
○ _____
○ _____
○ _____
○ _____
○ _____

**27** FRIDAY

○ _____
○ _____
○ _____
○ _____
○ _____
○ _____
○ _____
○ _____

**28** SATURDAY

○ _____
○ _____
○ _____
○ _____
○ _____

# November
## 2026

**29** SUNDAY

- ○ _____
- ○ _____
- ○ _____
- ○ _____
- ○ _____
- ○ _____
- ○ _____
- ○ _____

**30** MONDAY

- ○ _____
- ○ _____
- ○ _____
- ○ _____
- ○ _____
- ○ _____
- ○ _____
- ○ _____

## NOTES

_____
_____
_____
_____
_____
_____
_____
_____
_____
_____
_____

# December
## 2026

**01** TUESDAY

○
○
○
○
○
○
○
○

**02** WEDNESDAY

○
○
○
○
○
○
○
○

**03** THURSDAY

○
○
○
○
○
○
○
○

**04** FRIDAY

○
○
○
○
○

**05** SATURDAY

○ _____
○ _____
○ _____
○ _____
○ _____
○ _____
○ _____
○ _____

**06** SUNDAY

○ _____
○ _____
○ _____
○ _____
○ _____
○ _____
○ _____
○ _____

**07** MONDAY

○ _____
○ _____
○ _____
○ _____
○ _____
○ _____
○ _____
○ _____

**08** TUESDAY

○ _____
○ _____
○ _____
○ _____
○ _____

**09** WEDNESDAY

○
○
○
○
○
○
○
○

**10** THURSDAY

○
○
○
○
○
○
○
○
○

**11** FRIDAY

○
○
○
○
○
○
○
○
○

**12** SATURDAY

○
○
○
○
○

**13** SUNDAY

**14** MONDAY

**15** TUESDAY

**16** WEDNESDAY

**17** THURSDAY

○
○
○
○
○
○
○
○

**18** FRIDAY

○
○
○
○
○
○
○
○

**19** SATURDAY

○
○
○
○
○
○
○
○

**20** SUNDAY

○
○
○
○
○

**21** MONDAY
○
○
○
○
○
○
○
○

**22** TUESDAY
○
○
○
○
○
○
○
○

**23** WEDNESDAY
○
○
○
○
○
○
○
○

**24** THURSDAY
○
○
○
○
○

**25** FRIDAY

○
○
○
○
○
○
○
○

**26** SATURDAY

○
○
○
○
○
○
○
○
○

**27** SUNDAY

○
○
○
○
○
○
○
○
○

**28** MONDAY

○
○
○
○
○

**29** TUESDAY

○ _____
○ _____
○ _____
○ _____
○ _____
○ _____
○ _____
○ _____

**30** WEDNESDAY

○ _____
○ _____
○ _____
○ _____
○ _____
○ _____
○ _____
○ _____

**31** THURSDAY

○ _____
○ _____
○ _____
○ _____
○ _____
○ _____
○ _____
○ _____

NOTES

_____
_____
_____
_____

www.ingramcontent.com/pod-product-compliance
Lightning Source LLC
Chambersburg PA
CBHW052114020426

42335CB00021B/2754